Mondays Stink!

23 Secrets to Rediscover Delight and Fulfillment in Your Work

Carl Dierschow

Copyright © 2003 by Carl Dierschow

All rights reserved under International and Pan-American Copyright Conventions. No part of this book may be reproduced or transmitted in any form or by any means, electronic or mechanical, including photocopying, recording, or by any information storage or retrieval system, without express permission of the author, except for the inclusion of brief quotations in a review.

Published in the United States by Imprint Books Inc., www.imprintbooks.com.

ISBN: 1-59109-908-0

Illustrations by Daniel R. Brown.

The characters depicted in the stories are composites and examples, and in no way describe any specific individual. The characters depicted in the illustrations in no way describe any specific individual.

For additional information about the book go to the author's website: www.dierschow.com

Contents

Introduction ix

My Story xiii

Structure of This Book xv

Theme A: Create Your Support Group 1

1. Like and Respect Your Colleagues 3
2. Trust Others and Give People the Benefit of the Doubt 7
3. Communicate Openly With Anyone and Everyone 11
4. Seek Out People Who Appreciate What You Do 15
5. Try to Help Others Be More Effective and Look Good 19
6. Appreciate Everyone's Unique Contributions and Abilities 23
7. Set Appropriate Expectations 27
8. Actually Commit 33
9. Take Care of the Little Things Immediately 37
10. Build Bridges Rather Than Burning Them 41

Theme B: Take Care of Your Needs 45

11. Invest in Understanding Yourself 47
12. Look for Jobs That Align With the Organization's and Your Personal Goals 51
13. Stay With Organizations Which Have a Philosophy Compatible With Your Own 55
14. Understand Others' Points of View 61
15. Look at Every Activity as an Opportunity 65
16. Limit the Encroachment of Work on Your Personal Life 69
17. Keep Your Lifestyle Within What You Are Currently Paid 73

Theme C: Deliver Value to the Organization......77
    18. Focus Intensely on Delivering Value to the Organization.................79
    19. Expand Your Impact Whenever You Can.................83
    20. Do the Best You Can on Your Job.................87
    21. Take Responsibility for What You Should Own.................91
    22. Vocally Support the Organization's Goals.................95
    23. Choose Your Battles Carefully.................99

What Next?......103

How Healthy is Your Job Satisfaction?......107
    My Support Group.................107
    My Needs.................109
    Organization Value.................110

Improving Your Job Satisfaction......111
    Your Support Group.................111
    Your Needs.................119
    Organization Value.................125

Additional Resources......131

Introduction

> THE BIGGEST MISTAKE THAT YOU CAN MAKE IS TO BELIEVE THAT YOU ARE WORKING FOR SOMEBODY ELSE. JOB SECURITY IS GONE. THE DRIVING FORCE OF A CAREER MUST COME FROM THE INDIVIDUAL. REMEMBER: JOBS ARE OWNED BY THE COMPANY, YOU OWN YOUR CAREER!
>
> —Earl Nightingale, motivational speaker

At the beginning of the twenty-first century, our lives seem to be disappearing beneath a tidal wave of stress and overwork. We enjoy the highest standard of living in history, yet we feel that our fundamental human happiness is at an all-time low. Employees of large organizations feel this acutely, and they are worried their security, happiness, and value are controlled by others.

This trend has reached crisis proportions, and threatens the very existence of large organizations. American workers are in too short supply and have too many alternatives to be wasting their lives in unfulfilling jobs.

Unfortunately, it is impossible to return to the previous century when job security provided for each individual during the course of decades. Global competition is fierce and always increasing. The very existence of government and non-profit organizations is also being questioned. Pressure from small, nimble startups will force constant cost cutting and strategic rethinking. Significant functions are being restructured or outsourced.

Comfortable employment agreements for long-term job security between workers and their employers have permanently disappeared. Organizations are no longer able to afford this luxury in a time when cost pressures are constantly increasing.

For those who choose to recognize it, a new employment agreement is arising. Actually, it is not new at all—it always has been the way business works. The agreement is simple.

Organizations will attempt to keep the workers it perceives are the most valuable.

Simply stated, this means if you provide continuing value for your employer, you probably will be provided with job and learning opportunities during the course of many years. This is the way business works. Employers realize they have a significant investment in their employees, and business success always lies with retaining their top workers. The same is true for any organization that understands its workers are the way to accomplish its mission.

So where do you find job satisfaction? One-hundred years ago, only the wealthy few could expect to find any kind of fulfillment through their work. Fifty years ago, enlightened companies realized that continued employment with opportunities to contribute led to faithful, satisfied employees. Unfortunately, today's pressures on companies to break expectations of lifetime employment result in scared, overworked employees. Clearly this is a problem for large corporations that are losing their top contributors to alternate career choices or small, startup businesses.

This is an extremely complex problem for employers, and the solution is not obvious. Some are figuring this out, but many are not. As an employee, you can wait for the answer to appear by enduring the pain and suffering in the interim, or you can take action by addressing your own personal fulfillment needs within your organization.

The philosophy for doing this is simple.

You create your own job satisfaction.

This means you cannot rely on your employers to give you all the answers, if indeed they ever could. You need to take actions to ensure you have motivating work, enjoy the environment and your co-workers, and do not overwork yourself and ignore your personal goals. Peter Drucker explores this concept in his excellent article, "Managing Oneself."

Five years ago, I restructured my thinking and career planning around this principle, and the change was startling. During this time, my employer experienced increasing turmoil. I focused on my purpose and goals, and continued to be valued by my managers. For me, this yielded deep fulfillment—not only in my so-called "leisure" activities—but also on the job.

The secret to job satisfaction is simply the intersection between two simple concepts. The first is that **your employer needs value from you** or the organization will not be interested in giving you jobs and opportunities for growth. The second concept is that **you need things from your employer**—reasonable income, interesting jobs, worthwhile contributions, and stimulating learning opportunities. When you have these, you are likely to be a productive employee who is interested in staying with the company for the long term.

As these concepts intersect and align, we produce a win-win result for everyone. It is difficult to maintain this state of alignment during the course of many years, but it is well worth the effort. This is how you find purpose, stability, and happiness in your job.

Ideally, there should be a huge intersection between your needs and the company's needs. When this happens, you will find it is much easier to be energized by your work and the organization's values. You will have flexibility and continue to find interesting challenges for many years.

It is common for people to never feel as if they have found this "sweet spot." If you are experiencing stress and lack of job satisfaction, then this book is for you. It will give you some ideas, help you take control of your own job satisfaction, and create a win-win relationship with your employer.

My Story

THERE IS ONLY ONE SUCCESS—TO SPEND YOUR LIFE
IN YOUR OWN WAY.

—Christopher Morley, *Where Blue Begins*

Just as many people, especially men in the American culture, I never realized that delving into my inner being was particularly important. It's easy to define yourself by the roles you're assigned—employee, friend, spouse, parent. These roles easily can become the totality of your self-image.

My own breakthrough came with the convergence of a career turning point, a growing sense of unrest, and my deepening attachment to my church. It finally occurred to me that there might be something deeper I should do with my short time here on earth. I believe this is what many people might call a mid-life crisis.

For me, this was a wake-up call to search for my inner self. And sure enough, the universe handed me the right book at the right time—*Building Your Field Of Dreams* by Mary Manin Morrissey. I then launched on a path of self-discovery and introspection by describing my likes, dislikes, skills, and weaknesses. This became the basis for examining jobs that might bring me personal satisfaction.

Two years later, I delved into the process with the assistance of a gifted career coach. He used some simple tools to help me clarify my deeper values and interests, and ultimately, we described some jobs that I later investigated and even applied for.

These things don't change quickly. What I learned continues to help me. I now have a basis for seeing why I move toward some things and away from others, and for addressing certain areas of my job that frustrate me. For the first time in my career, I am making significant progress on my personal development that provides value to my employer and me. I don't know what my future holds, but I feel much more confident in my ability to be flexible and make the best of whatever life gives me.

I wrote this book because I want to reach people who feel powerless and dispirited in working for large organizations. For you, my message is simple: you *can* make a difference, and you *can* take control over what happens in your career.

Structure of This Book

The following sections in this book focus on three main themes:

    A. Create your support group
    B. Take care of your needs
    C. Deliver value to the organization

Within these themes are 23 independent ideas or "secrets," that are numbered sequentially. An assessment tool and a set of suggestions and actions follows the 23 secrets.

It is not necessary to read this book from front to back. If there are particular topics that interest you the most, feel free to read the appropriate chapters and the corresponding portions of the assessment tool, suggestions and actions. You will find these ideas are connected, so you may end up exploring the ideas in random order. Feel free to read it that way! This is your book, so use it in whatever way is most useful for you.

Use the final exercise to identify specific areas to work on and additional steps you can take to make tangible progress. It is probably best if you focus on only one or two areas at a time so you can see concrete results in a short time. You will gain energy by seeing quick results, which will help launch you into more significant work on improving your job situation.

Theme A: Create Your Support Group

The first enabler for a wonderful work experience is a supportive environment. You cannot act on your own within an organization: you affect many others in the company and need the help of a lot of other people.

Your first task is to build friendly work relationships, help others see the value you bring to the company, and create the opportunity for others to support you as an individual. This, of course, takes considerable time and effort. The payoff is that this can dramatically increase your ability to have some control over your freedom. Even if you end up with no more job control, working with a group of people who like and support you helps make work less stressful.

Creating a group of supporters is definitely within your control. You start with your managers, co-workers, and others with whom your job brings you into contact. As you change groups and jobs over the years, you have natural opportunities to enlist more supporters.

You also want to look for people who have unusual power and influence upon the larger organization. Find opportunities to work with them. Even volunteer for tasks outside the normal scope of your job. This greatly improves your chance for creating friendship and support.

1 | Like and Respect Your Colleagues

Gene and Charlie started working in the same group at about the same time. Gene was proud of his accomplishments, and this caused him to secretly believe the others in the group weren't as expert as he was. Over time, the others detected a subtle note of distance, and even superiority.

Charlie, on the other hand, was more

forward in expressing his gratitude for others' help. Even though he wouldn't have picked some of them as friends, he made sure he showed nothing but friendliness and support. As you might expect, the group ended up being closer to and more supportive of Charlie, and they went just a few steps further to help him through his challenges.

In addition, Charlie and Gene developed completely different views of what it was like to work in this group. Gene sensed a lower level of support, and he ended up feeling like an outsider. Charlie, on the other hand, enjoyed the experience and stayed with the group for several years because he liked the people.

To a large extent, Gene and Charlie both created their experiences in this group. What they gave to others was mirrored back to each of them because that is the way human nature works.

You start by creating a supportive attitude inside yourself. If you like your co-workers, you find everything else becomes much simpler because they help give you the energy you need to make other improvements.

You may not like everyone you work with or work for. But you can nurture a philosophy that each person deserves basic human dignity and—perhaps after some searching—has something to teach you. That is why liking and respecting people is a conscious choice: it is all about the attitude you choose to take about the people around you.

You will work for many bosses over the course of your career. Some are clearly in the wrong job. From those bad apples you can learn patience, compassion, persistence, and how to manage upwards. Observing bad decisions and overreactions, you can learn how to recover from mistakes and how to create environments for better decisions. The key point is to learn and grow regardless of your situation.

It is intriguing to note that challenging situations can help you learn more about yourself and the organization than you ever would have in a safe, comfortable environment. Even if you dislike someone, you can try to learn from them and build a relationship of support. If they exhibit disagreeable behavior, you can choose to value and respect them. You can support them when possible and resolve differences in a respectful way. You also can learn a great deal about the types of people with whom you work easily.

Is it political, inauthentic, or even hypocritical to treat your co-workers this way? Absolutely not. You do not have to compromise your own standards of excellence and honesty in order to treat others as likeable and worthy of respect. This is a basic, underlying philosophy about the value of people as human beings. Your response to specific situations will flow from that. If you disagree with others, fine, but handle it in a supportive way.

EVERY HUMAN BEING, OF WHATEVER ORIGIN, OF WHATEVER STATION, DESERVES RESPECT. WE MUST EACH RESPECT OTHERS EVEN AS WE RESPECT OURSELVES.

—U Thant

2 | Trust Others and Give People the Benefit of the Doubt

Linda felt like she was slowly becoming paranoid because her supervisor kept reducing her working hours. It felt as if she wasn't trusted or supported any more although she was one of the most experienced employees. Ultimately, she was let go.

Mondays Stink!

Her supervisor let Linda go partly because she had a habit of assuming the worst in every situation. When a co-worker came back late from a break, Linda thought it was because he or she was trying to sabotage the company. When Linda's supervisor had to reduce her hours due to declining revenues, Linda thought it was really because her supervisor didn't like her.

The supervisor saw this was affecting Linda's morale and everyone Linda worked with as well. She was giving a bad presence to customers so it was best to remove her from her job.

Unfortunately, this type of behavior is all too real. Linda was not making an attempt to understand why others did certain things. She jumped to conclusions that assumed the worst. Advice columns are built on people who assume that the universe is out to get them, nobody makes dumb mistakes, or that there are no different ways of looking at things. Sometimes it seems paranoia reigns supreme.

Most people do the best they know how based on their environment and what they think they are supposed to be doing. Mistakes and problems with adults usually arise from different goals and misunderstanding one another's situations.

If this is the case, then problems with others are not because the others are incompetent: it is because we do not share rich communication around common goals. And this is usually no one's fault. It is just the natural result of diverse people working in large organizations.

There are a number of tools that can help highlight the different approaches and goals of diverse people. Are you frustrated by others who cannot seem to understand what you are trying to say? Do others approach decision-making in different ways? Assessment tools, such as the Myers-Briggs Type Indicator® (popular in many large organizations), can help you compare your natural style with others and understand how to better communicate with others in your organization. Many other assessment tools are available—each with its own purpose and insight.

This concept of trusting others can be expanded to communities, countries, and even the world. Most of the conflicts we experience on the national and international levels do not exist because one party is right and the other wrong. It is because nations do not share a common view of what is right and wrong in the first place. This is why cultures and political systems are different. No particular system is inherently better or worse—they are each trying to achieve different goals.

This principle can be successfully applied to upper management and their decisions. Most managers are highly capable, motivated individuals. Many of the problems people have with management decisions is that they are based on a significantly different view of what is healthy for the organization and how success is measured. Sure, the way decisions are implemented often could be improved, but leaders' trade-offs between constituencies, customers, employees, and affordability present a huge challenge for even the most capable person.

Moving from giving people the benefit of the doubt to trusting them is not easy. It is possible to strive toward this by seeking to understand your colleagues, to avoid the trap of denigrating people to others, and to ultimately be openly supportive. When you do this consistently over time, you build bridges of trust.

When you understand others' points of view, you become much more tolerant of their behavior. You do not tend to assume the worst about others' contributions or treat problems as personal affronts. This can give you a great deal of emotional energy to expend on your own passions rather than spending it on things you cannot change.

> YOU MAY BE DECEIVED IF YOU TRUST TOO MUCH, BUT YOU WILL LIVE IN TORMENT IF YOU DO NOT TRUST ENOUGH.
>
> —Frank Crane

3 | Communicate Openly With Anyone and Everyone

When Anzo was first hired, it was clear he was a highly intelligent person and could bring a lot of value to the group. After several months, though, his co-workers realized they were always giving and never getting. The problem was that Anzo thought his value to the company came from being

smarter and more capable than the other employees. He would give information to his boss and others in power but he would hold it back from others he perceived as his "competition."

This created a large rift within the team. Others stopped communicating with Anzo because they weren't receiving much value from the effort. So Anzo became less effective and more frustrated. Eventually, he was moved to a different location because he didn't work well with his team.

Communicating effectively can be a big challenge because there are different ways of interacting in different contexts. The healthy approach is to be open and honest. This tends to be returned by others to create a stable, trusting relationship. Clearly, Anzo did not put any effort into developing an open, sharing relationship.

It is generally true that people value honesty, especially when they are brought together in teams to achieve a common purpose. This helps build confidence and openness in the team and results in efficiency and alignment.

Communication is a fascinating topic because many (perhaps most) "people problems" stem from faults in communication. Every individual has a different style of communication, yet we rarely modify our own style to adapt to that of others. Instead, we often assume that others understand and react to communication the same way we do. To help remove this blind spot, first examine others' styles and then change accordingly. Many assessments and excellent books are available to help you accomplish this.

Second, you should be as open and forthright as you can. This creates a large number of people who tend to trust you and your motives. They will tend to give you the benefit of the doubt when you make mistakes.

This gives you greater freedom to be self-managing and to chart your own career course within the corporation. You also will create healthy relationships with a number of people with whom you can discuss contentious issues without causing damage.

A manager needs to be aware of some special requirements. When unable to disclose some information, she or he should follow reasonable conventions about what to withhold. For instance, a manager might not be able to disclose significant decisions about a reorganization until the appropriate time. This makes sense because in this case employees must all be informed at the same time or in a certain order. When a good manager does communicate a tough decision, he or she does so honestly and openly, based on a solid understanding of the supporting context.

How should a manager communicate a decision he or she might personally disagree? First, understand others' points of view and the full context behind the decision. As was discussed in Secret 2, the decision-makers usually do have reasons and logic behind their actions. Second, it might help to communicate the process you personally went through to understand and support the decision. Third, if it is important not to communicate doubts and disagreements, don't. It is a matter of placing the larger, more important goals of the organization ahead of short-term disagreements. Of course, there also can be times when you believe you must stand true to your own principles and integrity. Just recognize you may be sacrificing your clout in the organization and negatively affecting others around you when you choose to enter battle with managers above you.

This is quite different from acting as if you support a decision with which you disagree. If you are merely acting, then there will be many ways (inflections, body language) your employees will understand you are not being authentic and honest. Typically, this will result in huge damage to the morale of the team and the credibility of the manager. And, it will place you even further behind than when you started.

A manager's display of cynicism can cause incredible damage. If it is important for employees to support something, then having their manager display lack of buy-in often will lead to organizational failure. In other contexts sarcasm, humor, and even cynicism can be acceptable as long as they do not lead to fracturing the organization. At times, they can be useful communication tools, but they are powerful and can do damage if applied improperly.

> THE MOST IMPORTANT SINGLE INGREDIENT IN THE FORMULA OF SUCCESS IS KNOWING HOW TO GET ALONG WITH PEOPLE.
>
> —Theodore Roosevelt, US President

4 Seek Out People Who Appreciate What You Do

Over the course of several years, Angela had the opportunity to work with a number of people in different groups. A few of these individuals became supportive friends who thought well of Angela's skills, attitude, and teamwork.

She experienced the normal ups and

> *downs in her career, but eventually she received chance to work for Frederic. Angela had mentored Frederic when he was new to the company many years ago, and he later was promoted to a position of considerable influence. He liked Angela as a person and knew firsthand from her mentoring that she had some solid experience and worked well in teams although she was quiet and under-valued by other managers.*
>
> *Frederic became Angela's best coach and adviser, and they worked well together for eight years until a reorganization took them in different directions. They continue their professional relationship informally, and they've acted as references for each other.*

Angela was smart in nurturing the support of Frederic. She understood the value of this as an asset, not only in her happiness when working for him but in strengthening her long-term career.

One step beyond having supportive work relationships is to have people who actively support you. To do this, seek out those who are strong supporters of you. These can be bosses, co-workers, employees, or even partners outside the company.

Having identified these people, try to keep contact with them over the course of your career. In the long run, this can present you with some surprising opportunities and some degree of protection and support during times of turmoil.

When you have a chance to work closely with these people, they will tend to give you a great degree of freedom in how you approach your job. You will be given more latitude to make contributions well outside your immediate area of ownership.

Every interaction is an opportunity to create a future supporter. Chance associations can result in positive experiences. They can be built into recognition for your contributions and value. That recognition can grow into identifying new opportunities for success that can blossom into active support for you to learn and advance. Just think: every wonderful relationship began as just the smallest interaction.

And conversely, relationships wither and die if you do not nurture them. Keep in contact with your supporters. Ask how you can help them. It is well worth the investment. And, use your supporters to further expand your circle of influence.

> DON'T WAIT FOR SOMEONE TO TAKE YOU UNDER THEIR WING. FIND A GOOD WING AND CLIMB UP UNDERNEATH IT.
>
> —Frank C. Bucaro

5 | Try to Help Others Be More Effective and Look Good

Matthew was one of the top performers in his division—productive, fast learner, hard working. Unfortunately, he made a point of promoting himself in front of others by giving the impression he had a larger role in his team's success than was true.

His teammates, one by one, began to

hold back from helping Matthew. Not in large ways, certainly, but in ways that mattered. From their point of view, it was only fair so they would get ample recognition for their own skills and contributions.

Matthew had a hard time figuring out why he felt more and more isolated. It's not that others were unfriendly or dishonest, exactly. . . . Work just wasn't as fun or easy as it was when he started. He transferred to a different group, and a year later, he started to have the same feelings again. He was inwardly miserable, even though his manager still valued Matthew's work.

We have all become weary and wary of people who shamelessly self-promote, even if their claims have some credibility. People who take this approach believe publicity is more important than contribution. Matthew fell into this trap, and he failed to make the connection with his teammates' negative responses. If he doesn't change the way he supports his team, he may become even more bitter and isolated.

A much better approach is to invest your efforts into recognition of the contributions of others and make others look good. They will tend to return the recognition of your value, sometimes to a surprising degree.

Many spiritual philosophies teach that good deeds will be returned many times over. Giving to others is a powerful way to attract support, directly or indirectly. Healthy trust is built upon people who are willing to support each other without expecting a specific return.

People will quickly sense if you praise meaningless contributions, so it is vital to be absolutely honest about this. You can help ensure people make important contributions by helping them be effective. If you are a manager this will be an important part of your role. You can play an important role in helping co-workers, partners, or your boss make true contributions and be more successful.

It is called giving to others with no particular expectation of receiving anything in return. Help others because it creates the kind of supportive environment where you would like to work, one where people energize and help each other.

Keith Ferrazzi is a master of networking described in *Inc.* magazine (Raz, "The 10 Secrets of a Master Networker," January 2003.) He draws amazing power and influence from actively building connections to people around the world. And one of his rules is "don't keep score." When you push too hard for an immediate return from a relationship, you fail in the long run. When you give generously of your time and help, others will want to be generous to you in the future. That is the way relationships work.

I'VE DISCOVERED THAT THE BUSINESSPEOPLE WHO ARE THE BUSIEST, THE HAPPIEST, AND THE MOST PROSPEROUS ARE THE ONES WHO ARE THE MOST GENEROUS WITH THEIR KNOWLEDGE AND THEIR EXPERTISE.

—Tim Sanders, Yahoo Chief Solutions Officer, in *Fast Company* magazine

6 | Appreciate Everyone's Unique Contributions and Abilities

Antoine was known in his company as a division manager who got results. He was a driver who forced people in his organization to deliver or leave.

The people who worked for him learned quickly what kind of management style was

effective. They rewarded actions that led to bottom-line results, and employees who failed to provide results were moved elsewhere or dismissed. This created a culture of fear and turnover.

Elizabeth was a first-level manager in Antoine's division who had a different philosophy. She recognized that a stable organization could deliver even more long-term value, so she made sure each employee in her group was personally valued for their uniqueness. When one skilled worker needed to work different hours to be at home at 3 p.m. for his children, Elizabeth adjusted the team's meetings. When another wanted to lead a key initiative for the team, Elizabeth supported her and helped smooth relationships with other affected teams.

Within six months, Elizabeth's team was known widely as the best place to work. The team not only gained some of the best results in the division, the manager knew how to accommodate her employees' needs and goals.

The corporate environment can be incredibly de-motivating because it tends to treat people as unimportant or as "assets to be managed" in the pursuit of corporate goals. This drains all the energy out of employees and leaves them unfulfilled. Antoine might have been able to get some short-term results at the expense of the long-term health of his organization.

An enlightened manager such as Elizabeth rejoices in the diversity of jobs, approaches, and values. Within a group's goals there are often many different ways to reach success. People who are supported will bring their full energies to a job and are more likely to get results than others who are less motivated.

Everyone wants to be recognized for their achievements and supported in doing what they think is best. It is not uncommon for others to have much better approaches than the manager suggested, especially within the context of their own abilities and expertise.

Often a "class system" develops inside companies. It is easy and uplifting to show appreciation to the many people who make our lives easier: the servers in the company cafeteria, the facilities crew who sweep the walks, and the people in other groups who may not realize they make your life easier. This attitude will be noticed by others and will slowly change your outlook on the value of everyone you meet.

> I BELIEVE THAT THE FIRST TEST OF A TRULY GREAT MAN IS HIS HUMILITY. I DON'T MEAN BY HUMILITY, DOUBT OF HIS POWER. BUT REALLY GREAT MEN HAVE A CURIOUS FEELING THAT THE GREATNESS IS NOT OF THEM, BUT THROUGH THEM. AND THEY SEE SOMETHING DIVINE IN EVERY OTHER MAN AND ARE ENDLESSLY, FOOLISHLY, INCREDIBLY MERCIFUL.
>
> —John Ruskin

7 | Set Appropriate Expectations

Patrick and Li worked in the same group on similar assignments. Patrick was viewed by their manager, Connie, as having the ability to do high-quality work since he was much more experienced than Li. Li had been on the job for about a year. She was certainly knowledgeable but not yet an expert. Li and

Patrick were both surprised when Connie gave Li the assignment to lead an investigation into a new opportunity for the business.

From Connie's point of view, Patrick was not as reliable as Li. Patrick could do good work and perhaps even faster than Li. But unfortunately, Patrick tended to work on assignments for days or weeks and then pop up with the results at the end. This made Connie nervous because a few times in the past Patrick missed important deadlines with no prior warning. When Connie inquired how an assignment was progressing, Patrick responded, "Things are fine, I'll get it done."

Perhaps Li's inexperience was one reason why she would keep Connie informed about the progress of her assignments, including the good news and the issues. So, paradoxically, Connie felt more in control of Li's work because she knew there would be plenty of warning if the issues were going to endanger Li's delivery of assignments. And on this new, risky investigation, Connie wanted confidence that issues would be highlighted and dealt with in an open way.

There is no doubt peoples' opinions of you are based on how they see your contributions and behaviors—and also are based on their expectations. No doubt you expect your children to do different things at different ages: your expectations with respect to their skills and maturity should rise over the years.

So it is in the workplace. Your colleagues, bosses, and partners all expect you to deliver a certain amount of work, with given quality, in a certain amount of time. The neat thing about the work environment is that we have influence over these expectations. This means we also can influence the resulting excitement or disappointment when we meet or fail to meet expectations.

This is not the same as the demands or requests made by others. Your boss might ask you to deliver something by tomorrow morning. But, he or she might not actually expect that request to be filled. The expectations will be based on your previous track record, how you responded to the request, and additional feedback received from you or others concerning the difficulty of the job, roadblocks, and opportunities.

Your track record is based upon peoples' perceptions of your previous work, which will probably be close to what you actually did. As people observe your actions over a period of time, they will have strong expectations for how you normally behave. Radically departing from those expectations will create surprise—either positively or negatively.

Other factors are easier to control in the short term. Whenever you accept an assignment, you have the opportunity to set the expectations. Chris received this e-mail:

```
From: Fred
To: Chris

Hey Chris,

Could you please get me a copy of
those quarterly reports by Friday?

Thanks,
Fred
```

It is obvious Fred expected Chris to give him the reports by Friday but Chris had a lot of unanswered questions about this request. What time Friday? A report summary or all underlying detail? In e-mail or paper form? What would happen if Chris was unable to produce the reports? These kinds of open questions can be time bombs waiting for Chris to seriously disappoint Fred or perhaps opportunities to exceed expectations. That is why it is so important to close the gaps with a 15-second response:

```
From: Chris
To: Fred

Fred, I can e-mail you the quarterly
report summaries by Thursday night,
no problem. If you need the detailed
spreadsheets behind them let me know
ASAP because it'll take a lot of
extra digging.

Chris
```

With this simple message, Chris took the chance to exceed expectations ("Thursday night, no problem"), clarified some open questions, and avoided a potential disaster regarding the detailed reports. It is also quite possible he avoided some unnecessary work.

This kind of conversation is very important, yet it is something we seem to have lost during the last decade. Fortunately, you have the chance to take control over misset expectations, and it does not take a lot of work.

Why wouldn't you want to always set expectations as low as possible so you can always exceed them? Well, because it damages your credibility and the peoples' perceptions of your reliability. The trick is to be able to pleasantly surprise people most of the time while having them see you as an honest and dependable person.

The other trap in setting expectations too low is selfmotivation: low expectations will result in low performance, little learning, and slow growth. Set commitments and expectations high enough that you are challenged to learn and improve, and not burn out.

UNDER PROMISE, OVER DELIVER.

—Tom Peters

NEVER PROMISE MORE THAN YOU CAN PERFORM.

—Publilius Syrus (~100 BC)

8 Actually Commit

For several years I had an interest in learning about personal coaching with the possibility of becoming a full-time corporate coach. I even talked to my bosses about this, attended a few seminars, and read some books. I didn't progress very quickly or in a clear direction.

So a few years ago, I signed up with a coaching university under a corporate coaching program. The change in my attitude was immediate and dramatic, especially when I declared to my manager that I had made this commitment. Suddenly, I had a clear direction. I promised myself to complete the training program and learn as much as I could.

When I changed groups, I talked with my new manager to ensure she also supported my investment in coaching. Partly because she saw the commitment I had to this area, she helped me expand my knowledge and contribution through coaching individuals and teams.

It is important to make commitments and live up to them. But there is a more powerful approach than just showing your employer how much work you can get done.

The critical impact of making a commitment is on *yourself.* When you are passionate about something, you do a better job, your productivity improves, and you have more fun. This commitment is something you control. It comes directly from how you *choose* to direct your attention and energy. You can even choose to commit to something you do not particularly like, and that will help give you energy and make it a less stressful experience.

There is also significant power in making your commitments visible to your boss, your workmates, your customers, and even yourself. The valuable role a personal coach can play is to capture your goals and commitments and keep them visible to you over time. Groups, such as Weight Watchers® and Alcoholics Anonymous®, use the power of the declaration of commitment, and can create truly life-altering experiences.

You do not need to like or be inspired by every aspect of your job. Everything we do is a combination of great and distasteful—that is part of life. But there is always some value you can get out of any job, and you can commit to getting the most out of it. This helps you to get through the hard and unpleasant times. Maybe you can learn a great deal about how to do the job, or enjoy the people you work with, or explore new skills. If you cannot find anything you can commit to, then commit to finding a new job. It will give you focus and purpose, help you overcome obstacles, and reduce your stress.

Consider two dark sides to making a commitment. First is the chance for failure. That is why you should concentrate on commitments that are truly important to you and will give you great value. That promise of value will help carry you through the hard work, problems, and barriers you will encounter.

The other dark side is that once you commit to something, it can be difficult to let it go. It is healthy to spend extra energy in these situations, and help yourself through the "separation anxiety" that comes from a job change or other shift in your focus. It is like a miniature grieving process that takes time and attention. This is a small price to pay for the extra energy you get from becoming committed to your tasks the rest of the time.

UNLESS COMMITMENT IS MADE, THERE ARE ONLY PROMISES AND HOPES... BUT NO PLANS.

—Peter Drucker

THE ACHIEVEMENT OF YOUR GOAL IS ASSURED THE MOMENT YOU COMMIT YOURSELF TO IT.

—Mack R. Douglas

9 | Take Care of the Little Things Immediately

Samer had been with the company for eight years and had been promoted to division manager. Unfortunately, his work day became busier and busier as he advanced. His days were often eleven or twelve hours of back-to-back meetings.

Subsequently, he got out of touch with

> *his people. He never seemed to have the time to attend to even the most minor of tasks and instead relied on his assistant to screen calls and direct him to the next meeting. He no longer made the time to ask people how they were doing or even say "thank you." Yes, he was working incredibly hard on those tough, strategic issues, but he was out of touch and burned out.*
>
> *The people in the organization felt less and less committed to Samer and to the organization overall. Turnover increased, and new-hires believed they had no management support and direction.*

Samer fell into one of the traps of popular time-management techniques: he concentrated so heavily on the big, important tasks he forgot about the people affected by his actions. An important trick to prioritizing your work that seems to be counter-intuitive: do some of the easy things first. (Allen, www.davidco.com)

Many time-management experts will teach that strict prioritization of tasks is the path to success: distinguish between what is urgent versus important. Then work on the most important things first, the ones that will have the largest impact. Of course, these are often the ones that take a lot of work and a long time to deliver. Important things are rarely easy.

Unfortunately, this does not account for peoples' expectations. Others expect hard things will take a long time, perhaps with pitfalls along the way, so they do not expect to see quick results. In addition, you usually do not have too many big activities underway at any time, so people expect that results of this work will be relatively infrequent. Increasing communication so they can see progress being made is important, but it is only one of the tools at your disposal.

The corollary to the previous statement is that others also expect the easy things to take a short time with few mistakes. So if you prioritize them behind the hard things, you will probably disappoint people often with tasks they thought were easy to do. This is a recipe for disaster.

Some people try to avoid small tasks by putting large barriers around themselves, such as not responding to e-mail or voice mail. Sure enough, this tells others you will not be responsive to the little things so they tend to go elsewhere. Unfortunately, this also gives a strong message that you do not want to be a valued member of the team.

The middle ground is to spend some time on the easy things. Say "thank you" for a contribution. Forward a message to someone who could get great value from it. Spend a minute asking "how are you doing?" Listen to the answer. The point is to do these things immediately so they do not enter into your time-management process. The benefit you get from doing this for some part of your day is huge: people want to interact with you, and they see you as attentive, responsive, and connected.

Do not queue up these small, simple things for several days because you will forget about them, and others will get the sense you do not care about them anymore. Do not bother tracking them on your time-management system because they come and go too quickly. They are often too trivial to track relative to your important long-term goals.

These small things are important. Not necessarily in the short term, to help you get your job done today, but in the long term. Attending to the simple things builds bonds of trust and generosity. It helps you create a group of people around you who you like to work with because they like and support you.

> IN ALL THE AFFAIRS OF LIFE, SOCIAL AS WELL AS POLITICAL, COURTESIES OF A SMALL AND TRIVIAL CHARACTER ARE THE ONES WHICH STRIKE DEEPEST TO THE GRATEFUL AND APPRECIATING HEART.
>
> —Henry Clay, US orator and politician

10 | Build Bridges Rather Than Burning Them

Leticia was devastated when she was laid off—it threw her entire life into disarray. She had only a few days to hand off her work to another person on the team. Unlike others in similar situations, she decided to make the best of these few days. She organized all her information, met with quite a few people who might be most

affected by her departure to address their concerns, and made it easy for her replacement to get up to speed as quickly as possible.

When the company was able to hire a couple of years later, everybody on the team immediately brought up Leticia's name. She clearly cared for their success, and was familiar with the group's tools and processes. So they called her and offered her a raise in order to get her back from the competition.

When Leticia left the other job, she was just as careful to prepare her replacements to be successful. Although they felt the loss of a good employee, they were able to quickly compensate and adjust.

Most people notice that over the course of many years, they tend to run into the same people over and over again. It is because they are in the same community, same company, common line of work, or have other overlapping interests. When you move to a different city and work for a different company yet continue these contacts over the course of decades, it can feel strange.

But, this phenomenon is an important asset to your career. During your lifetime, you will contact thousands, perhaps tens of thousands of people. If they have a good impression of you, it can open doors for future opportunity. If they are left with a bad experience, doors might close that you are unaware of. Leticia learned it is important not to damage relationships unnecessarily.

Being fired is a most unpleasant, life-altering experience. But if the manager treats you with respect and honesty, you may not harbor a lifetime grudge.

You might have heated disagreements with a co-worker. But if you are open to looking at their point of view and making the best decision to meet shared goals, it is much less likely they will avoid you in the future or disparage you in front of others. In fact, it might just form a bond of common respect.

Your company might hate a competitor, fighting to the death for market share. But if you treat their employees as humans worthy of respect, you may be able to forge a bond five years from now when the corporations merge and you now have to rely on one another for help. Or you might find you are able to hire the best and brightest from the other company because they like the way you treat people.

This phenomenon is entirely unpredictable, and it can bring excitement and joy to your life. Or you fear every change because of the possibility you will have to work with some of the enemies you created over the years. It is your choice.

> ALWAYS BE NICE TO PEOPLE ON THE WAY UP, BECAUSE YOU'LL MEET THE SAME PEOPLE ON THE WAY DOWN.
>
> —Wilson Mizner, screenwriter

Theme B
Take Care of Your Needs

While you are creating a supportive environment, you need to ensure you do not forget to nourish yourself: devote time to your goals, your values, and your life direction. If you neglect your needs, you will quickly run out of energy, and you will become an unfulfilled, unproductive contributor to your employer.

Caring for yourself is not as easy as it sounds! You face two challenges. The first is to become clear about your personal values and direction. At times, this may be difficult to separate from your role in the company, but it is crucial to know who you are and what brings you energy and happiness.

The second challenge is to find the right balance. Self-absorbed employees are not really what companies need: companies need people who can become committed to their jobs and corporate goals.

It is not really the true goal of an organization to give its employees satisfaction. Corporations primary goals are to deliver value, make money, and achieve strategic objectives. Inspired and happy employees are only a means to those ends, and only some companies truly understand this connection.

It is your job to look after your personal goals. If you do not do it, who will?

11 Invest in Understanding Yourself

Thomas was raised according to his parents' values and never really delved into self-understanding until he reached his thirties. At that point, he started getting a sense that there was a deeper purpose to his existence on the planet, beyond contributing to his employer and providing for his family.

He began a wonderful journey of discovery into spirituality, philosophy, and introspection. He hired a personal coach who helped him explore some goals that had been floating around in his mind for a number of years. One of these goals was to create sculpture. This exercised his creative energy in ways that would touch people emotionally.

Thomas explored changing careers, but he decided the government agency where he worked provided some opportunities to explore art. After about a year of laying the groundwork and investigating possibilities, he got a job supporting a museum. This was one giant step closer to creating his own works because he could associate with artisans who understood and supported him. At the same time, he was able to continue a decent income to support his family.

Thomas is happier than he's ever been. He's exploring and learning something new every day. He's not sure where he'll be in ten years, but he now has the flexibility to move in a number of different directions depending on opportunities that may arise.

Self-understanding is key to everything else in this section. If you do not understand yourself, then you will not be able to focus on the things that will bring you deep satisfaction.

A surprising range of resources and tools are available to explore your inner self: books, assessments, counselors and coaches, seminars, even close friends. It does not take a lot of money. It does take time and focus. And you will continue to discover more about yourself as you change and grow over time. This is a lifelong journey.

You might choose to approach your journey of self-discovery in many ways. You might ask yourself the following questions.

- Who is my true self?
- Why was I put here?
- What skills and abilities have I accumulated?
- What gifts have I been given?
- What is my niche?
- What is the one thing I want to accomplish in my life?
- What would give my life value?

Answers to any of these questions can bring great insight if you approach them honestly and openly. The key is to find an approach that gives you the most insight. Do not be surprised if it takes you in unexpected directions!

> TOO MANY PEOPLE DIE WITH THEIR MUSIC STILL INSIDE THEM.
>
> —Oliver Wendell Holmes

12 | Look for Jobs That Align With the Organization's and Your Personal Goals

José never got very inspired about his work. It was a job, it fed the family, but he never felt that it "connected" with who he really was. This went on for sixteen years, until he started questioning: is this all there is?

José hooked up with Sam, a career

coach, who helped him examine his true career goals and how to find his own direction. He ultimately changed organizations and learned a number of skills he never considered before. He has never been happier because he knows he's getting so much more out of his experience than just a paycheck.

And as José learns more about himself and his interests, he sees possible jobs he wants to go after in the future. He's building his skills and connections so he will be considered a prime candidate for those jobs when an opportunity opens up. He's having fun again.

José is finding the state of balance that you might be seeking. Companies attempt to keep the employees who deliver the most value to them. People would like to work for companies that offer them an environment that supports their personal goals.

You need to take an active role in seeking out jobs that get you closer to this balance. The ideal job for you:

- lets you build on your strengths and skills,
- gives you challenges you are ready for at this stage in your career,
- is highly valued by your employer, boss, and customers, and
- is in an environment and with people who give you joy and energy.

It is critical to believe such a job exists for you, even if you have to create it yourself. If you believe it right now, then work with a coach or self-development tools to get clear on what you truly want in your life. Describe the various jobs that might meet your needs and then start investigating them in more detail.

This also gives you the formula for creating your own job in an organization if necessary. Conceptually, it is rather simple.

1. Get clear and focus on what you need from and can give to a job.
2. Find specific decision maker(s) who are willing to work with you.
3. Find out what would bring them so much value they would be compelled to give you the freedom to do something unusual.
4. Create an implementation plan and sell it to the key sponsor(s) based on delivering this compelling value.
5. Work with the sponsor(s) through all the organizational barriers to success.

This process is not trivial or quick, but you can use it to custom design jobs for yourself. It might take years of investment, but the payoff is huge: you may gain a job for which you are uniquely adapted and totally dedicated.

This is the life you were given, and no one can tell how much you might have left. How important is it to find a career that truly fits your life goals? How much work is it worth to find, or even create, this career?

IN ORDER THAT PEOPLE MAY BE HAPPY IN THEIR WORK, THESE THREE THINGS ARE NEEDED: THEY MUST BE FIT FOR IT; THEY MUST NOT DO TOO MUCH OF IT; AND THEY MUST HAVE A SENSE OF SUCCESS IN IT.

—John Ruskin, English writer

13 | Stay With Organizations Which Have a Philosophy Compatible With Your Own

Evelyn moved from job to job over the years and never really found a compatible group. This was frustrating. She thought her career was going nowhere.

During a team-building exercise, she gained an opportunity to work on

understanding her personal values. The results "clicked" like never before. She discovered that she really wanted to make a difference for disadvantaged persons in the community. She had been volunteering at her church to help out with the local soup kitchen, but it never seemed as if she was making a significant difference to the community.

She thought she'd have to leave the safety of her employer and perhaps reduce her income substantially in order to meet this deep need. On a whim, she started to explore the crucial question: Is there any place in this company where they also are focused on helping the disadvantaged people? The results astounded her.

She found opportunities in the human resources department and worked with employees who were having trouble in the corporation—the individuals who have disabilities and those who earned only minimum wage. She connected with a person at headquarters who was responsible for philanthropy in the community. And, she found a group of people who were working on daycare alternatives for new mothers.

Even more important than the jobs these people were doing, however, was the culture they created within each of their groups. They were focused on respect for

*and the welfare of individuals. She
contacted these different groups, and when
an opening came up, she took a starting
position in human resources. She's never
been happier.*

Each corporation, agency, or association has its own culture. Within them, each group or organization has its specific culture. Often this is set by the philosophy of the person who manages it. The particular industry and mission of the group also influences the culture. Today, we even find global trends that influence the flavor of industries, companies, and teams.

Your job satisfaction stems from many places. One key factor is whether you constantly run into conflicts with the basic philosophy of the people you work with on a daily basis. Describe your own philosophy, and then compare it with the group culture to see if there is a match. Evelyn put some effort into understanding herself, and she took a much different and satisfying career direction as a result.

How can you understand the true culture of a team when you are interviewing? It is not as hard as you might think, especially if you have access to people who currently work in the group. Usually, they will give you an honest assessment since they are concerned about how well they will work with you in the future. And, you always have the right to ask interviewers about the goals and nature of the team you might want to join.

Sometimes there will be such huge differences you find you cannot be happy in a company. When this happens, it is time to move on. Define your goals and start searching for possibilities. Search out groups that have values similar to your own and individuals who like and support you. You might even turn down job offers because of their organization, and that is OK.

Finding a group that works for you can greatly reduce one source of stress in your life. It makes you a more valued employee to the organization since you tend to be happier, more energized, and consequently, more productive. When you find a compatible group, plan to stay, even if you have to change jobs to do it.

It can be important to continue with an organization long enough so you can figure out how it really works. Some people jump from job to job after staying only for a couple of months. This might be necessary in some cases, but it can be damaging to move around too often. How can you figure out how an organization really functions in such a short time? How can you become productive at a complex job? Employers who see a pattern of job-hopping will shy away from hiring you or at best will be reluctant to invest in your long-term success.

In the end, your judgment and inner feelings play an important role in deciding when to switch jobs, either within a company or from one organization to another. You have to balance your current level of satisfaction and effectiveness with progressing toward your long-term goals and ultimate career objectives. This balance is different for each person, so do not expect another person's answer to be the same as yours.

Never doubt that a small group of thoughtful committed people can change the world: indeed it's the only thing that ever has!

—Margaret Mead

14 | Understand Others' Points of View

Bruce had just moved from the finance department to marketing, and he was having problems adjusting. Marketing didn't seem to care at all about creating procedures, much less in following them, but this had been his area of expertise in his prior job. He felt lost. He sometimes felt like he was

speaking a different language to his new teammates.

He found help in a colleague, Sonia, who moved from marketing to manufacturing a couple of years ago. Sonia felt a similar kind of disruption in her move, so she really cared about helping Bruce with this problem. She was able to describe the culture of marketing in an outsider's language, and even suggested some language he might want to use in group meetings. She didn't get everything exactly right, of course—several key people had moved on, and Bruce's experience was a little different. But, she helped Bruce look at the different values in the marketing group and question some of the assumptions he had made based on his experience.

Bruce continued to work on this culture-shift as his top priority. Several months later, he successfully made the adjustment and was feeling included and productive. He even became a liaison with his old finance group because he was able to translate between the two team cultures.

The larger an organization gets, the more problems are created by miscommunication. This is one reason why small, focused groups are still the best tool for making progress. The more people interact, the more they understand one another's points of view. They may not agree with or subscribe to that point of view, but at least they understand it. So when you hear or see a message, immediately put it in the context of your understanding of the other person's context.

Fortunately, Bruce recognized he did not understand the culture of the marketing team and sought some help. Sometimes a personal coach also can help decode confusing situations such as Bruce's.

When you do not understand another person's situation and context, you tend to adopt these views.

- Whatever they are doing is not as valuable as what I am doing.
- They seem to be doing their job the wrong way.
- They make unreasonable requests of me.

Conversely, when you try to communicate to another person where you do not understand their situation and context, you can easily make these mistakes.

- You state things in words that are not easily understood by the recipient.
- You try to explain things in ways that do not fit with their understanding of how things should work.
- You make requests that might seem reasonable to you, but perhaps you fail to make sense to them.

This is why it is so important to understand another person's context. It is relatively easy to apply to the co-workers you meet daily, but the concept is just as important when you communicate with people in other departments, across the country, in other parts of the world, and even in management.

We tend to quickly dismiss management's statements as meaningless, incomprehensible, or just plain wrong. Management people take their jobs just as seriously as we take ours, and they usually are trying to do the best they know how. Managers live in a much different context than workers: they are measured on and are rewarded for different things, and there is a whole different language and way of looking at success. When you see how that works, then it is much easier to understand why managers act the way they do and what they are trying to achieve.

The same holds true for your co-workers across the country and world. They usually have different goals than yours, and their norms of communication and decision-making can be quite different. Even in a common organizational culture, there are significant local variations. Before judging the actions of others, try your best to understand their culture and environment. This usually has a big impact on your ability to understand and support what they need from you.

> SEEK FIRST TO UNDERSTAND, THEN TO BE UNDERSTOOD.
>
> —Stephen R. Covey, *The 7 Habits of Highly Effective People*

> ALL TRUTHS ARE EASY TO UNDERSTAND ONCE THEY ARE DISCOVERED; THE POINT IS TO DISCOVER THEM.
>
> —Galileo Galilei, Italian scientist

15 Look at Every Activity as an Opportunity

Rose was given an unpleasant assignment. She was to be involved in decisions about how to reduce expenses in the department. She knew this would mean painful squeezing of purchases, travel, and possibly even the loss of jobs. She didn't know how these sorts of decisions got made. All she knew was that it was painful for everyone involved.

Once she acknowledged the decision was made, she started looking for a silver lining to this dark cloud. She figured out that this experience might help her possibilities for future promotion since it would involve her directly with some of the toughest decisions. She also would get direct hands-on experience with analyzing the budget. Possibly she could find ways to change some impediments to team success while saving money, such as the way decisions were made about travel. Certainly, if she did a great job, it would encourage her manager to view her as valuable employee.

This also helped her build her enthusiasm around this assignment so she could put in the hard work necessary to do a good job. And, she worked with her boss to act as the key decision-maker and communicator so she wouldn't be rejected by the rest of the team for the impact of the budget cuts.

Every job is a balance between good and bad experiences. One way to get through the painful parts is to find what you can learn from the experience. This gives you hope that your skills will improve over time, things will get easier, and you will deliver more value to your group.

Rose knows every job is an opportunity to make a contribution. Certainly, if a company invests money to create your job, someone believes there is value in it. When you are unclear about the value of your contribution, it is uplifting to find out who created the doubt. Often, it is your boss. Talk to him or her about how you could improve the value of what you do. When discussed in an open and honest manner, the manager usually will see you as an energized employee the group's best interests at heart. You will learn a lot about how you can improve your real and perceived contributions.

The more control you have over your work, the more you can design it to give you opportunities to learn new things. This extends well beyond the technical aspects of your job, to working with people, communication, self-management. The list of opportunities is endless. When you are growing a little bit every day, the cumulative impact from year to year can be huge.

Finding and creating opportunities to learn is quite different from letting others dump all their unwanted tasks on you. The former is for the purpose of learning and developing. Over time, it will become natural to seek out more tasks in areas that you believe will contribute to your career. Once you see how to do that, then the next step is to change your existing work so it enhances your opportunities to learn and grow. Then ultimately you may have the chance to sculpt your own job description in such a way that it delivers maximum value both to you and your employer. (Butler and Waldroop, 2000) This process is described further in Section 12: "Look for Jobs That Align With the Organization's and Your Personal Goals."

OPPORTUNITY IS MISSED BY MOST PEOPLE BECAUSE IT IS DRESSED IN OVERALLS AND LOOKS LIKE WORK.

—Thomas A. Edison, inventor

16 | Limit the Encroachment of Work on Your Personal Life

I finally landed the perfect leadership job. I was building a new organization, working on important issues, and making a difference in the company. Unfortunately, the job came with a price. It consumed my every waking moment. With laptop PC, cell phone, and pager, I felt like every minute was at the demand of others.

> *The feeling of being indispensable was exhilarating for the first year. Then, it started to wear thin. I tried to limit the time I spent on work tasks during weekends, but on Monday mornings I felt like things were that much more difficult.*
>
> *I knew I was in trouble when I awakened, shaken and sweating, at 3 a.m. on a Sunday morning worrying about work.*
>
> *I realized I had created this monster through my own behavior. I had only two choices: either re-create my current job so I could live with it, or leave the job.*

It is incredibly important to establish your personal limits. Most salaried jobs in the United States have no protection against working a huge number of hours, and most companies would be very happy to get as much work from each employee as possible. Despite this being short-term thinking, that is how corporations measure their success. You need to look out for your long term.

Don't think it's just the number of hours worked. Some people are happy working 80-hour weeks, others with 20. Each of us are given different bodies, energy, and interests. You need to start by understanding who you are and what you have to work with. Next, you must establish a balance between giving to others and giving to yourself. You look for this balance point based on your different objectives, such as contributing to the world, your family environment, and even your own spiritual development.

Then, you can focus on managing your store of attention and energy. Fortunately, it is possible to replenish both. For some, it is going to the gym or reading every day. For others, it might be a lunch hour uninterrupted with work concerns. It might be the precious time with your kids between dinner and bedtime.

Whatever brings you physical and emotional energy, build it into your schedule and honor it as a top priority. Protect it. Nourish it. If you have to temporarily do without, then compensate for it before and after.

Yes, this might conflict with your job. That might mean you need to look for a new job, or negotiate to change your existing one so it will work around your personal priorities. In the end, if you give up your life and soul in exchange for a job, you will not be satisfied with the choice.

> *In the end, I ended up leaving that job, although I still work for the same company. The experience I got was invaluable, but I decided I'm not going to do that same kind of work again—it came at too high a personal price.*
>
> *Instead, I've focused my energies on creating a job which nourishes my personal goals while delivering value to my employer, and on writing a book to help bring what I've learned to others in similar situations.*

17 | Keep Your Lifestyle Within What You Are Currently Paid

Max was not one to flaunt his status but he did enjoy his position and the regular raises. Over a number of years, he and his family acquired a beautiful home, nice cars, televisions in every room, and all the other

things that come with American life in the twenty-first century.

As he aged, he started to feel locked in by his own possessions and lifestyle. He felt guilty about not really saving enough for a great retirement, which now seemed ever closer. And he felt hemmed in by the payments on his house and the amount of spending his family enjoyed. He wanted to explore other careers that potentially brought less income but he worried it would let his family down if he pursued them.

He finally had to face this conflict when his company eliminated his position. Working with a financial counselor and his family, they examined their lifestyle and eliminated a significant amount of expense. Not just for the short term, but for the rest of their lives. The family was surprised to find that this helped refocus them on being with one another rather than chasing the never-ending goal of consumerism.

This secret is a tough one for people in our culture. Money underlies a great number of family problems. Max has made significant progress but he has not totally eliminated this conflict.

We tend to measure success in the United States by looking at money: your salary, your net worth, or the value of all your acquisitions. The appearance of wealth draws people to expensive cars and houses, and rampant consumerism.

It does not have to be that way: we have the ability to choose what we will make important in our lives. If your goal is to be a multi-millionaire, great. People can find many ways to become wealthy in the twenty-first century. Just realize this is your choice. and no one is forcing you in that direction. Understand whether it is your true life goal, or if you are just using money to keep comfortable and isolated from your deeper life mission.

It might be useful to examine your current income, expenses, and savings for future happiness. Many financial planning resources are available to help. Distinguish what expenses are truly necessary, such as adequate food, housing, and transportation from everything else you spend.

Then, study these extra expenses with a critical eye. We view many things as necessary when, in fact, they are not. What was your lifestyle as a student? How would you live if we were plunged into a deep recession or world war? What are the critical things you would save if your house was burning down?

Some people become so clear on this they go even further, such as looking at the lifestyle of living in another country or state, or perhaps downsizing their house to something considerably more modest.

Living within your means, despite the difficulty of resisting social pressures, frees you to make decisions that are based on your needs and values more than on just money. It means you might be able to turn down a

Mondays Stink!

promotion because you would not be happy in the job. You may not have to wonder when the next pay raise might come. You might be able to take some time when you are unemployed to really find the ideal job.

You may find that the things that are most important to you do not depend on the size of your paycheck.

> Wealth is not of necessity a curse, nor poverty a blessing. Wholesome and easy abundance is better than either extreme; better for our manhood that we have enough for daily comfort; enough for culture, for hospitality, for charity. More than this may or may not be a blessing. Certainly it can be a blessing only by being accepted as a trust.
>
> —Roswell D. Hitchcock

Theme C
Deliver Value to the Organization

An organization values those people who are giving it the most value. This is merely the company's enlightened self-interest. You can take advantage of this fact by understanding what the organization values, delivering substantial value, and connecting with others to maximize the impact of your work.

This is a very simple, and crucial, concept. The word "value" means much more than just "doing your job," because it focuses on the higher level of understanding and contribution. Employees who understand and deliver what is truly important to a company will be valued most, and the first to be retained during tough times.

18 | Focus Intensely on Delivering Value to the Organization

The managers viewed Grace as a strong contributor to the organization. She responded to requests rapidly and was conscientious about the quality of her work. Over the years, she found that she seemed to be missing out on the truly exciting

opportunities, such as leading-edge, high-impact, high-visibility projects.

After discovering she hadn't been considered as a possible candidate for the latest leadership project, she had a frank discussion with her boss. To her surprise, she found out that she was viewed as a great follower but not necessarily a leader. Although she made great contributions to her group, other groups and managers didn't know much about her because she didn't directly impact their success.

Grace's experience is quite common, especially in large companies. The organization can get so caught up in day-to-day execution that this becomes a substitute for long-term, big-picture thinking. Many workers become distanced from decision-making and focus instead on doing their jobs as defined.

In general, this works well. After all, somebody has to address the day-to-day needs of the business, but it can become a disadvantage to your career. It can place you in a well-defined box, perhaps even a box that becomes irrelevant over time. You have to actively identify where the organization is going, and hone your skills to be ready for changes and opportunities when they arise.

For many people, this is a daunting prospect. After all, how do you figure out where the business is headed when the decision makers do not seem to know? How do you get in with the "in crowd" when they see no point in spending time with you?

Fortunately, it is not as complex as that. You do not have to be smarter than the bosses, you just have to understand what they are talking about and learn what is valued and rewarded. You do not have to be in the "in crowd" itself, you just need to watch what they are doing and find things to help with what they might value.

If your group's current priorities are to save money, then look for ways to eliminate expenses that would help the business succeed. If the priorities are to gain influence in the company, then look for ways to highlight successes to that broader audience, things the company would view as successful. If the priorities are to deliver customer value, then find out what the customers are asking for and look for ways to give that to them better than in the past.

Find out what is valued and how your organization defines success. Discuss the future directions with senior decision makers. Relate that to your job and your immediate group, and increase your efforts in that direction. Expand your view to find opportunities to help the business succeed.

Now, let's find out what happened to Grace....

19 | Expand Your Impact Whenever You Can

After the previous eye-opening discussion, Grace pressed her manager further. He told her most leading-edge projects began life as a spark of inspiration rather than through the normal planning process. She found that discussions with certain key "thought leaders" in the organization would help her

find and create opportunities to contribute when ideas were in formation.

Grace worked with her boss to identify specific ways she could contribute to other teams and the larger business. She didn't have much time to invest because of the demands of her normal job, so she focused on a few areas that were most interesting to her and appeared to have high potential value for her division.

She set up weekly informal talks with a couple of influential people, Benjamin and Terri. Usually these conversations were over a cup of coffee in a relaxing setting. Surprisingly, she found that Terri valued the opportunity to talk with someone who was well versed with the day-to-day work, who would be supportive, and would not challenge her in front of her management team.

Grace and Terri spent some time talking about how to redesign the way customer inputs were handled, and a couple of months later the division manager decided to staff an investigation in the area. Because of a recommendation by Terri, her personal interest, and some good thought put into the subject, Grace became the top candidate and was selected to lead a small team.

Grace finally figured out, with the help of some mentors, how to make a larger difference to her division. Although it will not be easy, she is excited about the new challenges and opportunities to make a difference.

One way to expand the value of your current job is to focus on decision-making two or three levels above you. Depending on your current location, this may be the upper-management level, or an internal group, division, or function. Do not focus on visibility for its own sake: focus on learning, understanding, and applying your creativity. Quietly watch and listen until you have a good feeling for what is most important to those people, and then create opportunities for increasing your contribution at that level.

Ideally, it would be best to have the support of your boss in doing this. Even without that, it may be possible to increase your scope of focus and attention. Plus, if you help your manager to be seen as a stronger person by other managers, he or she will probably ask for your help again and further expand your scope of influence.

The key is to focus on the larger picture by making a contribution to the larger organization outside your immediate team and current job definition. It helps a great deal to learn how to communicate in the language of your boss and other leaders and to help them understand the impact you provide them.

You also can expand your sphere of influence by working in different jobs. Actively go after new job openings that would allow you to learn new areas and connect with more people. Find ways to give others information that will help them succeed in their jobs.

> A LIFE IS NOT IMPORTANT, EXCEPT IN THE IMPACT IT HAS ON OTHER LIVES.
>
> —Jackie Robinson, athlete

20 Do the Best You Can on Your Job

Mahmood knew he was an expert analyst, but he was troubled because others didn't seem to see him that way. Sometimes he would get into long discussions with others about alternative analysis methods, which, it seemed, wouldn't yield as good a result.

He got to the point where he seriously wondered if he had a future with this corporation. Fortunately, a co-worker pointed him to a senior analyst, Barbara, who could act as a mentor. After some tough discussions, Barbara was able to explain the significant difference between being an analysis expert—what he had learned in school and from previous experience—and being a great analyst for this company.

One valued skill was to do "quick and dirty" analysis, to help test alternatives for decision-making. Mahmood learned that a thorough job really had no value if it couldn't be delivered on time or was so complex that people couldn't understand it easily. Barbara helped coach him around specific quick-turnaround jobs, and he found he really could do them well, based on his experience and intuition.

Mahmood had difficulty understanding the difference between doing a great job and delivering the most value for his organization. The business need was not just for the best analysis he could perform, instead it needed different kinds of analysis at different times. When he adjusted to this reality, he increased his value to the company.

It pays to understand what the organization really needs and to put effort into becoming an expert at your job. You need to get up to speed as quickly as possible, and then stay around long enough in the job to yield value. The challenge is to figure out how long is the right amount for you, so you do not stop learning, become bored, or burn out. It is an individual choice based on your own work patterns and personal preferences.

When you do stay in a job for a longer period of time, make sure you keep up with changes. Even over the span of six or twelve months, a job might change significantly or the environment around it might change. Just because you have the same job title as a few years ago does not mean you are doing the same thing.

Entrepreneurs who own small companies tend to understand their company's survival depends on understanding what customers need and delivering it better than the competition. But an employee hidden down inside a large corporation can easily become disconnected from this reality by focusing more on day-to-day tasks than what truly serves the customer. The result is that companies become slower and more inwardly focused as they grow further away from the customer and being competitive. This is dangerous for the future of large companies and corporate America.

Each of us plays a role in the success of our employer, and if we do not deliver true value we will lose the reason to be employed.

People who are good at their current jobs tend to be given promotions and increased influence. After all, few managers would take the risk of increasing reliance on somebody if that person was known as a poor contributor. Instead, they will wait for you to get good at your current job before giving you more responsibility. If you want promotions and influence, take care of your current job first.

The bottom line: quality matters. Do good work. Be fast and consistent. Fix your mistakes quickly. Recognition and results will come.

> Whatever is worth doing at all, is worth doing well.
>
> —Philip Dormer Stanhope, Earl of Chesterfield

21 | Take Responsibility for What You Should Own

Jake worked for me several years ago and delivered great work. But, he avoided conflicts. So when anyone needed something fixed, Jake was reluctant to address it. Over the span of several months, his co-workers realized it was easier to fix problems by

> *themselves rather than by asking him to redo his work.*
>
> *Jake sensed something was wrong and wondered why people seemed to value his contribution less and less. Teammates didn't ask him for help, even when he could have provided valuable assistance. Sometimes he would deliver something that never seemed to be used by anyone. Jake was frustrated and lonely.*

Jake's view of the organization was that mistakes should never happen and admitting fault was showing weakness in front of others. He is still struggling with this issue and seems unwilling to admit his mistakes to others.

The reality is that things change, mistakes are made, and miscommunications happen. You cannot run away from this just because it is uncomfortable. You must address situations quickly so life can move on.

People tend to have a surprising tolerance for flaws and mistakes. After all, each of us is painfully aware of our own shortcomings and problems. If you take responsibility for your actions and fix problems quickly, you can often be seen as more valuable than those who never made mistakes. It is counter-intuitive, but true.

The difference between doing a bad job and making a mistake is whether you correct it and learn from the experience. If you are constantly correcting your mistakes and making new ones, that means you are learning and growing. If you are making the same mistakes, it is time to step back and examine your fundamental approach and underlying assumptions. Perhaps you need help from others to find a different way to solve the problem.

This is also valid at the group or even the corporate level. The IBM culture is famous for the philosophy of taking responsibility for customer satisfaction, whether or not it was IBM's fault. IBM recognizes that respect from customers is worth far more than the ability to place blame and pass the buck. Customers do not expect companies to be flawless, but they do expect and even demand that problems be addressed quickly.

In 1982, Johnson & Johnson experienced a crisis when bottles of Tylenol® were laced with cyanide in Chicago. The company was saved when they took quick, decisive action to correct the problem by recalling products from shelves across the country. The public was shaken about the initial deaths, but the true character of the company was shown by how they reacted to and corrected the problem. Other companies that try to avoid responsibility for problems suffer enormously, and often go bankrupt over issues that could have been corrected.

> LOOK IN THE MIRROR TO ASSIGN BLAME, LOOK OUT OF THE WINDOW TO ASSIGN PRAISE.
>
> —Robert Hughes, Coach

22 | Vocally Support the Organization's Goals

Several years ago my organization was struggling with some big changes in our industry. After a time, employees divided into two groups: those who supported change and those who resisted it. I found when I talked with the change resisters that my personal view of the future became more

limited and more pessimistic. My own doubts and fears were magnified with no solution in sight. If I dared to mention something I agreed with, my point of view was soundly devalued.

When I talked with the change supporters, my future opened up to more possibilities. My fears could be addressed with people who wanted to help me fix the problem.

For me, the choice was clear: I chose to spend most of my time with the supporters, futurists, and positive thinkers. I talked openly about things I agreed with, which helped others who were struggling. I discussed my doubts, and the others helped me to address them. Ultimately, I made a significant impact on the change our division was undergoing.

For better or worse, our culture seems to reward conflict and negativity. At times, it can be difficult to speak positively about what is going on during times of tension.

You have a choice. If you think and speak supportively about the future, you will help build it for you and your organization. If you build up barriers and problems, then the future will overrun you.

There is another way to think about this. Suppose to your left is a co-worker who sees everything in a negative light: they hate their job, they don't like the company, their future is bleak. On your right is another who is supportive and positive. They see value in their job, they like working for the company, the future is full of possibilities.

Who would you like to hang out with? Why?

The person on your left is constantly draining energy from you, and the person on your right is feeding you energy. If you need your energy to overcome challenges and remain enthusiastic about your job, then you better not waste time with those who drain it.

It is easy to feel like a victim when you are a single employee in a large organization. Many things are beyond your control. But acting like a victim is a choice you make every day. Acting out victimhood is self-reinforcing and affects those around you.

The paradox is this: when you feed others with positive energy, you do not lose it yourself. In fact, you are likely to gain energy yourself because of the attitude of others around you and the positive future you are building inside your mind.

There is something incredibly powerful with communicating this positively to others who listen. It makes it more real, more tangible. You will see great opportunity and lead change when you bring out your positive energy.

FEW THINGS IN THE WORLD ARE MORE POWERFUL THAN A POSITIVE PUSH. A SMILE. A WORD OF OPTIMISM AND HOPE. A "YOU CAN DO IT" WHEN THINGS ARE TOUGH.

—Richard M. DeVos, Amway founder

23 | Choose Your Battles Carefully

Anya is absolutely passionate about the use of color in the work environment. She read a number of studies on the subject and tried hard to get her managers to repaint the walls and get new furniture.

The problem is that nobody else has any interest in the topic. The current market

conditions are very tight, and no one else sees why it's important to spend money on cosmetic fixes or replace furniture that is quite serviceable. Her boss tells her there is no money budgeted for such things.

Anya is becoming frustrated and is working even harder to sell her vision of a beautiful workplace, but it only creates more anxiety. Her boss tells her to stop talking about it because the discussions are creating too much friction.

Anya needs to understand that there is always an appropriate time and place for each battle. In this case, there are clearly more important issues in the organization than repainting the walls, and it is going to be extremely hard—perhaps impossible—to change those priorities.

And her managers may be entirely correct. They may have to make the choice between Anya's proposals and letting someone go. Clearly the business does not need this distraction right now.

There are several ways Anya might handle the situation.

- She could be patient, gather data, refine her arguments, and wait until the time is right.
- She could find an influential decision maker in the organization who is inclined to champion this idea.

- She could move to a different organization or company that is more supportive of her ideas.
- She could work on removing barriers for her idea, i.e., removing the cost by changing the color only when the walls were to be repainted anyway.
- She could try to start small by influencing the environment only for herself or her immediate work group.

Any of these approaches are valid, depending on the situation. The point is that Anya can change the battle from being unwinnable by focusing on a different problem or different approach.

When it comes to Anya's career, this decision can have a big impact. If she continues on the present course, it might even limit her future with the organization. The battle should promise a pretty big payoff!

By redefining the challenge, Anya has the opportunity to create a win for both the organization and herself. If something gets approved, even a first step, then she has the opportunity to be the leader to carry it forward. And in a few years, she may even see her vision come to life.

The bottom line: focus on those things that will give the greatest value to the organization as well as to yourself. You will experience alignment, support, and energy.

> Pick battles big enough to matter, small enough to win.
>
> —Jonathan Kozol

What Next?

Does this sound familiar?

> *Dear Seth: My company is filled with people (all of whom seem to be above me on the corporate ladder) who refuse to let us try anything new. Everyone at my level knows exactly what to do to save the company, but no one above us will let us. What should we do?*
> *-- Ethel Binder, Williamsville, New York*

Dear Ethel: What you're looking for is an insurance policy that will protect you against retribution if your plan goes awry. What you're waiting for is someone way up the ladder to tell you that you can launch a product or institute a cost-savings plan. You want their approval to free you from risk. That's not going to happen.

Just do it. If you wait for approval, it means that you want someone to cover your backside if you fail. The people higher up on the corporate ladder are well aware of the risk that comes with trusting you and your bellyaching associates. If you and your colleagues screw up after receiving their approval, then it will be your bosses who get into the deepest hot water, not you.[1]

---

[1] Reprinted from the November 2001 issue of Fast Company magazine. All rights reserved. To subscribe, please call 800-542-6029 or visit www.fastcompany.com.

Perhaps you are reluctant to begin creating the work success you want. Decide to start taking action. That is the easy part. Now, it is up to you to make the decision to begin.

The chapter, "How Is Your Job Satisfaction," contains a simple exercise you can use to determine areas where you might want to focus your efforts based on your perception of your current situation. Start with only one or two areas. The following chapter, "Working on Your Job Satisfaction," contains a number of actions you should consider taking in order to start making improvements. Finally, "Additional Resources" lists references that might be valuable to you.

On the following page is a development plan template you can use to focus your energy on specific steps you will plan to take. Or, feel free to use some other format.

Now is the time to get going!

> REMEMBER, PLANNING YOUR CAREER IS UP TO YOU, NOT YOUR FIRM. IF YOUR NEW CAREER PATH DOESN'T WORK OUT, THE RESULTS WILL BE A LOT MORE PAINFUL FOR YOU THAN FOR YOUR FIRM.
>
> —David H. Maister, *True Professionalism*

Personal Development Plan

Improvement Area	Learning Objective	Learning Steps	Resources	Timeline	Measurable Result
One of the 23 Secrets	Desired behavior improvements	Specific actions I need to take	People and tools I will need to use	When steps will be achieved?	How will I know each step has been successful?
•	• • •	• • • • •	• • • • •	• • • • •	• • • • •

How Healthy is Your Job Satisfaction?

Fill out the following survey to rate your skills on creating a job environment that excites, motivates, and supports you. In order to get an honest assessment, try to come up with specific examples of actions you have taken—not just your good intentions.

Then identify those areas where you rated yourself lower. Select the one that most interests you, and start working on it. A number of ideas are suggested in the next chapter.

My Support Group

1. I like and respect my colleagues:

Not at all	Some of the time	Most of the time	Almost always

2. I trust others and give people the benefit of the doubt:

Not at all	Some of the time	Most of the time	Almost always

3. I communicate openly with anyone and everyone:

Not at all	Some of the time	Most of the time	Almost always

4. I seek out people who appreciate what I do and how I work:

Not at all	Some of the time	Most of the time	Almost always

   I try to work with those people during the long term:

Not at all	Some of the time	Most of the time	Almost always

5. I try to help others be more effective and look good:

Not at all	Some of the time	Most of the time	Almost always

6. I appreciate everyone's unique contributions and abilities:

Not at all	Some of the time	Most of the time	Almost always

7. I set appropriate expectations with my boss and co-workers: | Not at all | Some of the time | Most of the time | Almost always |

8. I actually commit to others and to myself: | Not at all | Some of the time | Most of the time | Almost always |

I treat those commitments seriously: | Not at all | Some of the time | Most of the time | Almost always |

9. I take care of little things quickly: | Not at all | Some of the time | Most of the time | Almost always |

10. I try to build bridges rather than burning them: | Not at all | Some of the time | Most of the time | Almost always |

I actively try to rebuild damaged relationships that might be valuable: | Not at all | Some of the time | Most of the time | Almost always |

Overall, I feel supported and nourished by the people I work with or have worked with: | Not at all | Some of the time | Most of the time | Almost always |

My Needs

11. I invest in understanding myself: | Not at all | Some of the time | Most of the time | Almost always

12. I look for jobs that align with the organization's and my personal goals: | Not at all | Some of the time | Most of the time | Almost always

13. I stay with organizations that have philosophies compatible with mine: | Not at all | Some of the time | Most of the time | Almost always

14. I try to understand others' points of view: | Not at all | Some of the time | Most of the time | Almost always

15. I look at every activity as an opportunity to make a contribution and to learn something: | Not at all | Some of the time | Most of the time | Almost always

16. I limit the encroachment of work on my personal life: | Not at all | Some of the time | Most of the time | Almost always

17. I keep my lifestyle within my current income: | Not at all | Some of the time | Most of the time | Almost always

Overall, I tend to take care of my needs: | Not at all | Some of the time | Most of the time | Almost always

Organization Value

18. I focus intensely on how I can favorably impact the business: | Not at all | Some of the time | Most of the time | Almost always |

19. I expand my impact whenever I can so that I become more and more valuable to the organization: | Not at all | Some of the time | Most of the time | Almost always |

20. I do the best I can on my job: | Not at all | Some of the time | Most of the time | Almost always |

21. I take responsibility for what I should own: | Not at all | Some of the time | Most of the time | Almost always |

22. I vocally support the organization's goals: | Not at all | Some of the time | Most of the time | Almost always |

23. I choose my battles carefully: | Not at all | Some of the time | Most of the time | Almost always |

Overall, I focus on delivering value to the organization: | Not at all | Some of the time | Most of the time | Almost always |

Improving Your Job Satisfaction

After filling out the survey in the previous chapter, identify one area you believe additional work would give you the most value. Look that up in the table below where you will find a few suggestions for how you can strengthen your skills in that area.

If you also wish to work on a second area of development, fine—but make sure you focus on each one for sufficient time so that you will make substantial progress. It is much better to make significant progress in one area than to feel guilty about neglecting two.

Your Support Group

1. Like and respect your colleagues.

    - Focus on one person with whom you have the most difficulty.
    - Identify three good qualities in every person in your workgroup.
    - Identify the specific sources of conflict and create an opportunity to talk with the other person openly about them.

2. Trust others and give people the benefit of the doubt.

- Seriously evaluate the relationships with people with whom you have the lowest level of trust. Is this based on their actions or on your perception of them?
- Challenge yourself to analyze a situation where someone caused you to have negative emotions. What did they think they were trying to do? Why was it logical to them?
- Figure out how much of a risk you would really be taking if you decided to trust a person with whom you currently have difficulty.
- Read some books and articles on "emotional intelligence" to help understand how to relate to people with different views and approaches.
- Take an assessment as an individual or with your group to help understand styles, strengths and weaknesses with yourself and others. You receive valuable feedback from 360-degree assessments, which gather information from a number of points of view around you.

3. Communicate openly with anyone and everyone.

- Slowly increase your level of openness and honesty, and test to see how it is received by each individual.
- In a situation where you are asked to support something you do not feel good about, dig deeply into the issue. Why do others support it, and what is their frame of reference?
- Identify three people with whom you would most want to have an open and trusting relationship, and start opening up to them. Be honest about some of your doubts and weaknesses, and be supportive when they do the same.

4. Seek out people who appreciate what you do and how you work.

- Identify the people who supported you in the past, and try to figure out why they did.
- Look for, and perhaps invent, opportunities to work with those people again, even in an informal way. Rebuild the lost relationship.
- Talk with your supporters about whether those opportunities can be turned into a more formal job arrangement that would benefit you both.
- Recognize the contributions of others in ways that are appropriate to the culture of your group. Every day, send an e-mail of appreciation to someone and their boss. Mention your gratitude for others' help at group meetings. And keep doing this every day until it becomes habit.

5. Try to help others be more effective and look good.

- Identify the people you are reluctant to support in front of others, for whatever reason. Find or create opportunities to say something specific and supportive.
- Watch how your positive support comes back to you either directly or indirectly.
- Describe your current underlying philosophy about the value of and your need for self-promotion. Be honest and probe deeply.

6. Appreciate everyone's unique contributions and abilities.

- If you have leadership responsibilities, look for the places where those on your team have skills or approaches that you are not using for greatest value. Discuss this with them, and explore ways to expand this to contribute to team success.

- Find or create ways to discuss the value of diverse approaches in your team.

- Identify three people outside your immediate team every day for a week whose help or contribution you appreciate. No matter how small, find a way to express gratitude.

7. Set appropriate expectations with your boss and co-workers.

- Examine your achievements over the past few months, and identify those places where you either did not meet, or surpassed expectations. What could you have done to actively set expectations closer to what you actually delivered?
- Take time to question and understand the expectations of the person who assigned your next three tasks that cannot be handled in just a few minutes. And, also consider the people who will use the results, if they differ.
- At the next three appropriate opportunities, state something that will set a proper level of expectation, and thereby test to see if there is a significant gap. Adjust and negotiate, as you deem appropriate.

8. Actually commit to others and to yourself.

- Identify the places where your sincere commitment would deliver the most value to yourself and your organization.
- Explore what barriers you have to make a full and sincere commitment in those areas, to learn about yourself, and to find ways to increase your ability and desire to commit.
- See what happens when you speak of your internal commitment to someone else as an expectation or even a promise. How did you approach the task? Did it give you more focus or energy?

9. Take care of little things quickly.

- During the next week, identify any task that will take less than a few minutes of your time. Do those tasks immediately, if possible.
- After that week, analyze where this approach worked and where it didn't. How did it make you feel? How did it make others feel?
- Create a set of questions you should ask yourself to separate small –and unimportant tasks that you can ignore from the small but valuable ones. For instance, ask is this a relationship I want to nurture, and does this align with my team's purpose?

10. Build bridges rather than burning them.

- Identify places where you have burned bridges, intentionally or not. Be honest. Are any of these in areas that you would like to rebuild?
- Examine the behavior patterns that get you into trouble in this area. If you believe they are too deep for you to fix, find someone who can help and advise you. Learn how to change your patterns.
- Identify areas where your bridges might be shaky. Find people in those organizations with whom you can (re)build a trusting relationship.

Your Needs

11. Invest in understanding yourself.

- Work with a coach or someone who will agree to focus on honesty, openness, and hold your best interests at heart. Explore your goals, values, attitudes, and behavior patterns.
- Pull together all the feedback you have received in the workplace—from managers, peers, friends— and look for patterns. Dig into the areas you feel most uncomfortable, especially if you heard similar feedback from different people.
- Start a journal or diary, and explore your life's purpose.

12. Look for jobs that align with the organization's and your personal goals.

- Write down your personal and career goals, and review and refine the list every few days until you have something that feels powerful to you.
- Find and write down your organization's goals. Test with others to see if you understand them properly. Then write down three goals of the organization that no one wrote down because they are deeply ingrained in the culture or perhaps not "safe" to say.
- Look for positions inside or outside your company that align with your goals. Ignore salary and title for the moment. Evaluate what attributes of those jobs have good alignment, and those that do not. Use this to refine your understanding of your true goals and needs.
- Create three radically different job descriptions (they do not even have to currently exist) that would align with your personal goals. See how you can increase their value to the organization.

13. Stay with organizations that have philosophies compatible with yours.

- Capture your personal philosophy about life and work, perhaps with the help of a coach or trusted friend.
- Look for organizations anywhere in your company that might have some attributes that align with your philosophy. Find out more about them.
- Take time during the next month to ask questions that will help you more deeply understand the culture of organizations with which you come into contact.
- Do not be afraid to leave a situation in which you are deeply unhappy. This can be the best way to free up your time and attention to focus on what you really need.

14. Understand others' points of view.

- Find an area of the business with which you are confused or nervous. Investigate, and find out what others know that you don't.
- Identify an interaction with somebody where you are confused or nervous. Investigate to uncover the other person's point of view.
- Target a key relationship that you would like to build but is not yet established. Spend most of your interaction time listening and trying to understand. Delay giving your point of view.

15. Look at every activity as an opportunity to make a contribution and to learn something.

- If you are bored or uninspired by your current job, focus on how you can build up the value that you might get if you focused on learning, building key relationships, or doing top-notch work. What could excite you? How can you create that excitement?
- The next time you are uninspired by a task assignment, explore what a truly excellent result might do for your boss, your organization, and yourself. How could the value of that work be dramatically increased?
- Identify three areas where you have the ability to change something significant. What would happen if you were able to achieve much better results with much less work? Pay attention to whether this motivates and excites you.

16. Limit the encroachment of work on your personal life.

- Identify one thing you could do that would reduce the amount of time or effort you spend worrying about your job when you are not at work. Experiment with this for a month to see if it makes a difference.

- At the end of your work day, write down the list of things you do not want to forget tomorrow. Put this in a prominent place where you will be guaranteed to see it. Do this for a month to see if it helps you leave your work at the office.

- When you come up with a work-related idea or concern outside your work day, write it down and put it in a place where you will see it the next day. Leave yourself a voice-mail message at the office if that works for you.

- If you are working in a home office, establish regular office hours and stick to them. Do not attend to non-emergency work items outside your established hours. Do not check your e-mail or voice mail outside your hours.

- As an experiment, put a hard limit on the amount of time you spend working. Ruthlessly prioritize the work, and look for ways to get the most value from your limited time. Learn from this, and make permanent changes to the way you approach your job.

17. Keep your lifestyle within your current income.

- Seriously analyze your financial situation, including all debts and assets. Enlist the help of a financial adviser to learn how financial planning works.
- Tightly monitor your expenses for a week. You will be surprised at where the money goes, and this will help you set better priorities.
- Consider what would happen if you cut back your monthly expenses by 10, 20, 40 percent. How would you change your spending if you expected to be out of work for more than a year? Use this technique to help establish what is fundamentally important to you, your life's goals, and your family. There should be several levels of importance.
- Establish financial goals you and your family can agree with, and understand the limits that these things might put on your desired lifestyle. Identify areas where you might want to increase spending time rather than spending money.

Organization Value

18. Focus intensely on how your contribution can favorably impact the business.

- Write down your organization's goals on several levels, if that is appropriate. Work with knowledgeable people to make sure you truly understand the stated goals.

- Then, write down three goals of the organization that no one has written down because they are deeply ingrained in the culture or perhaps not "safe" to say.

- Identify how your job contributes to as many of these goals as possible. And, list two ways you would want to shift your job to provide even more value. Discuss this with your manager.

19. Expand your impact whenever you can so that you become more and more valuable to the organization.

- Identify three ways others could get more value from the work you already do. Investigate whether this would be valued by others as well.
- Talk to your manager about how you could be more valuable to the company. Be sincere about your desire to contribute. Explore shifting your responsibilities, doing things in a different way, and improving certain skills.
- Explore with some trusted teammates how you could deliver a better result from the overall team. Explore switching some responsibilities, changing processes, and building knowledge and skills you might need.

20. Do the best you can on your job:

- Work on actively setting expectations for the quality and timeliness of your work. Seek to usually meet, and sometimes exceed, those expectations.

- Set a specific goal for yourself to measurably improve your work within the next six months— enough that others will notice and be pleased by the improvement. Work toward the goal of being the best you can at your job.

- Discuss with your manager your sincere commitment to improve your contribution in specific ways. Ask them for honest feedback and help, and then hold them to that commitment. Be sure not to be critical of their comments and advice. Understand others' points of view and learn.

21. Take responsibility for what you should own.

- Explore any areas you can find where others hold you accountable for things, but you resist. Identify the core cause of the conflict and what you can do about it.
- For a week, attempt to never blame something on someone else. Find a different way to frame the issue so that it opens the door to your influence or control. At the end of the week, evaluate whether this change made a difference for you or other people.
- Find an area where you could take ownership of something that would have value to the organization. Investigate how you could make this happen without negatively impacting any one else.

22. Vocally support the organization's goals.

- Identify three areas you most strongly support the organization's stated goals. Without mixing negative information with positive, figure out how you could honestly answer, "Why do you support that goal?"
- Identify three forums, groups, meetings, discussions, where it would be appropriate for you to mention your support of an organizational goal. Set for yourself an objective to actually do it, and see how people respond.
- Vocally challenge others' cynicism in a constructive way. Search for ways to explore the sources of their cynicism, and change the point of view in order to find the underlying logic and rationale.
- Understand how you detect the difference between authentic enthusiasm and faking. Make a list of words, phrases, or actions that indicate whether a person is or is not being authentic. Increase your usage of the ones that seem most useful and genuine for you.

23. Choose your battles carefully.

- Identify three times you chose the wrong time to fight a battle. List the situation, outcome, and how you could have known in advance you would lose.
- Identify three times you have lost, but you considered the issues worth the fights anyway. Be clear about why it was worthwhile. See if you can identify ways you could have reduced the negative impact of losing the battle.
- Identify three times when you fought a worthy battle and won. Besides the outcome, why did you consider it worthy? What else did you get out of it? See if you can find ways you could have reduced any negative impact on other people.
- Identify three times when you won the battle, but in the end, it was not worth it. Examine the larger costs to yourself and others. How could you have known in advance it was not worth winning the battle?

Additional Resources

Books

Bardwick, Judith M. *Danger in the Comfort Zone: From Boardroom to Mailroom—How to Break the Entitlement Habit That's Killing American Business.* Saranac Lake, New York: AMACOM Books, 1995. ISBN: 0-814-47886-7.
www.amanet.org/books

Bernstein, Albert J. and Craft, Sydney. *Dinosaur Brains: Dealing With All Those Impossible People at Work.* New York, New York: Ballantine Books, 1996. ISBN: 0-345-41021-1.
www.randomhouse.com/BB

Butler, Timothy and Waldroop, James. *Job Sculpting: The Art of Retaining Your Best People.* Cambridge, Massachusetts: Harvard Business School Press, 2000. ISBN: B-000-05REH-L.
www.hbsp.harvard.edu

Covey, Stephen R. *The 7 Habits of Highly Effective People: Powerful Lessons in Personal Change.* New York, New York: Free Press, 2003. ISBN: 0-671-70863-5.
www.franklincovey.com www.simonsays.com

Forster, Mark. *Get Everything Done and Still Have Time to Play*. Lincolnwood, Illinois: Contemporary Books, 2001. ISBN: 0-658-02150-8.
www.mhcontemporary.com

Fortgang, Laura Berman. *Living Your Best Life: Discover Your Life's Blueprint for Success*. New York, New York: Tarcher/Putnam Books, 2002. ISBN: 1-585-42157-X.
www.laurabermanfortgang.com
www.penguinputnam.com

Gallwey, Timoth. *The Inner Game of Work: Focus, Learning, Pleasure, and Mobility in the Workplace*. New York, New York: Random House Books, 2000. ISBN: 0-375-75817-8.
www.randomhouse.com

Hill, Napoleon. *Think and Grow Rich*. New York, New York: Fawcett Books, 1990. ISBN: 0-449-21492-3
www.naphill.org www.randomhouse.com

Hubbard, Elbert. *A Message to Garcia*. Mechanicsburg, Pennsylvania: Executive Books, 2002. ISBN: 0-937-53965-1.
www.executivebooks.com

Johnson M.D., Spencer and Blanchard, Kenneth H. *Who Moved My Cheese? An Amazing Way to Deal with Change in Your Work and in Your Life*. New York, New York: Putnam Publishing Group, 2002. ISBN: 0-399-14446-3.
www.whomovedmycheese.com
www.kenblanchard.com www.penguinputnam.com

Kaufman, Barry Neil. *Happiness Is a Choice*. New York, New York: Fawcett Columbine Books, 1994. ISBN: 0-449-90799-6
www.randomhouse.com/BB

Leonard, Thomas J. *The Portable Coach: 28 Surefire Strategies for Business and Personal Success*. New York, New York: Scribner, 1998. ISBN: 0-684-85041-9.
www.simonsays.com

Levoy, Gregg. *Callings: Finding and Following an Authentic Life*. New York, New York: Three Rivers Press, 1997. ISBN: 0-609-80370-0.
www.randomhouse.com

Lynch, Dudley and Kordis, Paul. *Strategy of the Dolphin: Scoring a Win in a Chaotic World*. New York, New York: Fawcett Books, 1990. ISBN: 0-449-90529-2.
www.randomhouse.com

Marcum, Dave; Smith, Steve; Khalsa, Mahan. *BusinessThink: 8 Rules for Getting It Right—Now and No Matter What!* New York, New York: John Wiley & Sons, 2002. ISBN: 0-471-43066-8.
www.wiley.com

Morrissey, Mary Manin. *Building Your Field of Dreams*. New York, New York: Bantam Books, 1997. ISBN: 0-553-10214-1.
www.marymaninmorrissey.com
www.randomhouse.com/bantamdell

Rohn, Jim. *7 Strategies for Wealth and Happiness: Power Ideas from America's Foremost Business Philosopher*. New York, New York: Prima Publishing, 1996. ISBN: 0-761-50616-0
www.jimrohn.com www.primapublishing.com

Rohn, Jim. *The Art of Exceptional Living.* Niles, Illinois: Nightingale-Conant, 1994. ISBN: 0-671-50588-2
www.jimrohn.com www.nightingale.com

Ruiz, don Miguel. *The Four Agreements: A Toltec Wisdom Book*. San Rafael, California: Amber-Allen Publishing, 1997. ISBN: 1-878-42431-9
www.miguelruiz.com www.amberallen.com

Senge, Peter M. *The Fifth Discipline: The Art and Practice of The Learning Corporation*. New York, New York: Currency/Doubleday, 1994. ISBN: 0-385-26095-4.
www.randomhouse.com/doubleday

Stanley, Paul D. and Clinton, J. Robert. *Connecting: The Mentoring Relationships You Need to Succeed In Life*. Colorado Springs, Colorado: NavPress, 1992. ISBN: 0-891-09638-8.
www.navpress.com

Magazine Articles

"The 10 Secrets of a Master Networker," Tahl Raz. *Inc. magazine*, January 2003.
www.inc.com

"Managing Oneself," Peter Drucker. *Harvard Business Review*, July 2000. www.hbsp.harvard.edu.

"Change Agent," Seth Godin. F*ast Company magazine*, November 2001.
www.fastcompany.com

Organizations

Cheryl Richardson, www.cherylrichardson.com

CoachVille, www.coachville.com

David Allen Company, www.davidco.com

International Coach Federation, www.coachfederation.org

Ken Blanchard Companies, www.kenblanchard.com

Living Enrichment Center, www.lecworld.org

Tom Peters Company, www.tompeters.com

YourTrueNature.com, www.yourtruenature.com

Acknowledgments

I would like to start by thanking Gayla and Bob, who gave me the original inspiration to turn my random disorganized thoughts into a book.

I was graced to have a wide range of reviewers and advisers: Bobbie, Carmen, Carol, David, Dean, Deb, Deborah, Diane, Donna, Dwight, Jayne, Jeff, Laura, Monty, Philip, Sam, Sue, Terri and Terry. Thank you for keeping me on track and giving such wonderful advice! And thank you to my editor, Susan—your attention to detail is quite amazing.

Of course this book was drawn from a wide range of personal experiences over the course of my corporate career. I'd like thank all of my managers from whom I learned so much: Olin, Alvin, Wes, Sandy, John, Chris, John, Larry, Robert, Bob, Chris, Jim, Chris, Cristina, and the many others who have slipped my mind at the moment.

My co-workers and employees over the years are too numerous to name, but I give you my thanks for your support during my career. I have learned so much from you, including the joy of making a contribution through work.

I would like to thank the coaches I've worked with in recent years. Sam, you helped me to create a career that is truly based on creating a fulfilling life.

Finally, and most important, I thank my wife, Nancy, and our children, Lisa and Bryan, for the wonderful support you've given me during this adventure.

About The Author

CARL DIERSCHOW lives in Fort Collins, Colorado. He graduated from the University of Colorado with a bachelor's degree in software engineering, and has worked for several companies and a government agency in the United States and Australia over the span of some thirty years. Over half of this was as a first- and second-level manager in various capacities.

In addition to being a full-time corporate employee, Carl also is a trained Certified Comprehensive Organizational Coach. He is applying those coaching skills every day in his job, using this as a means of creating his own career fulfillment.

Carl is involved with his church, and finds that these spiritual experiences help him to be a better coach and employee.

About The Illustrator

DANIEL R. BROWN grew up in Huntington Beach, California. He graduated from Colorado State University in Fort Collins, Colorado, with a Fine Arts degree concentrated in Graphic Design. Daniel is a freelance illustrator specializing in hand-drawn cartooning.

You can contact both via the author's website at www.dierschow.com.